Pop it o...

Written by Suzannah Ditchburn
Photographed by Will Amlot

Collins

It is a top.

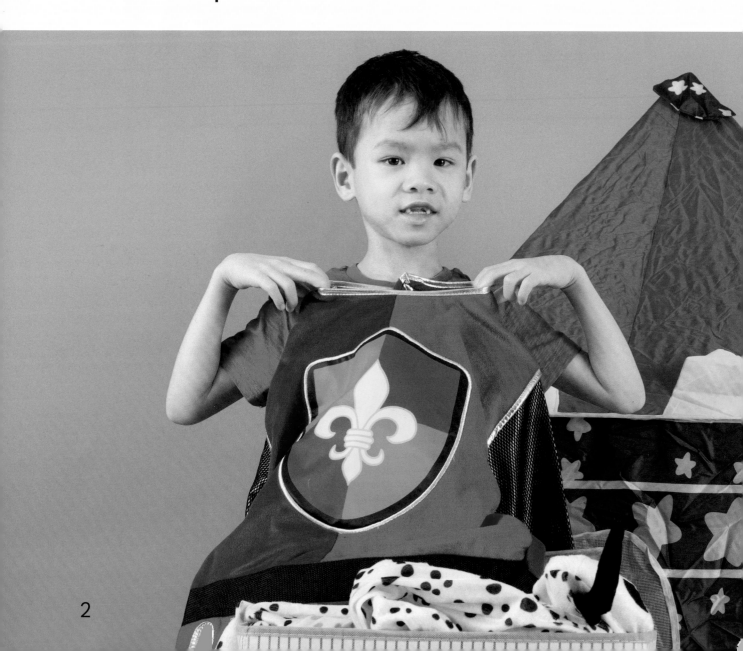

Dom pops it on.

It is a map.

It is a pot.

Sam pops it on.

It is a pan.

A dog.

dog tag

8

Sit! The dog sits.

Sam taps the pots.

tap tap tap

dots

The dog sits.

The dog is sad.

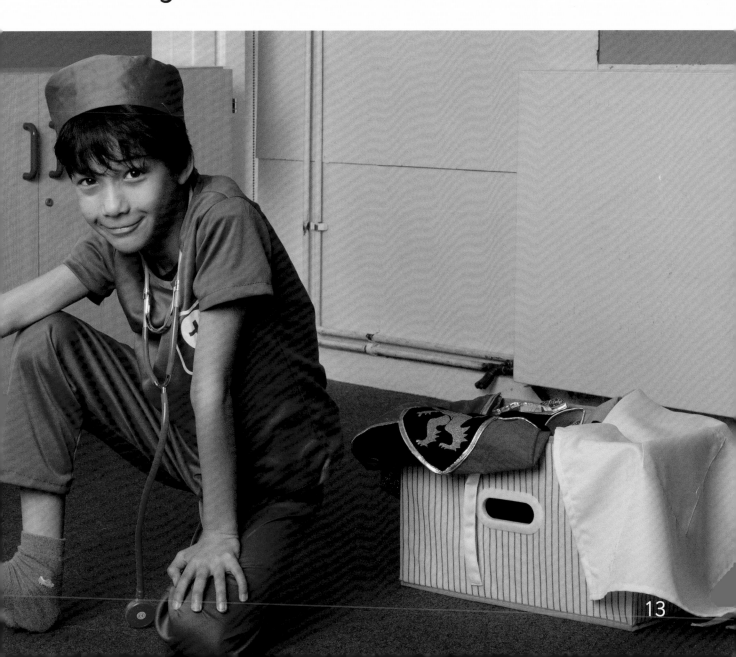

15

🐾 Review: After reading 🐾

Use your assessment from hearing the children read to choose any GPCs, words or tricky words that need additional practice.

Read 1: Decoding

- Turn to pages 2 and 3. Point to **pops** on page 3. Ask the children to sound out the letters, then blend. (*p/o/p/s* – **pops**) Ensure they don't miss out the /s/ sound at the end. Ask the children to read **is** on page 2. Can they hear that the "s" has a different sound in **is**? (/z/)
- Take turns with the children at pointing out words to sound out and blend. Sound a letter out incorrectly once or twice, saying: I'm not sure that's right? Encourage the children to correct you.
- Look at the "I spy sounds" pages (14–15). Say: I can see lots of things that have the /o/ sound. Point to the fox hat and say "fox", emphasising the /o/ sound. Ask the children to find other things that contain the /o/ sound. (*donkey, dog, blobs, octopus, pop, oranges*) Do the same for the /g/ sound. (*grapes, glasses, gift bags*)

Read 2: Prosody

- Choose two double page spreads and model reading with expression to the children. Ask the children to have a go at reading the same pages with expression.
- Discuss how you point to the object that is labelled as you read the label.

Read 3: Comprehension

- For every question ask the children how they know the answer. Ask:
  - On page 2, what object does "it" mean? (*the top*)
  - On pages 4 and 5, how do we know these children are pretending to be explorers? (e.g. *their clothes, their map, the monkey, the magnifying glass, the treasure pot*)
  - On page 8, which words are the labels and what do they point out? (*the dog tag*)
  - On pages 12 and 13, how is the dog feeling? (*sad*) What has the boy on page 13 popped on? (e.g. *vet's clothes; a hat, uniform and stethoscope*)